Letting Go... Holding On:
Surrendering to Life As It Is

Letting Go...Holding On - Surrendering to Life As It Is
Copyright © 2018 Anne Lesley Lanier

All rights reserved. No part of this book may be reproduced (except for inclusion in reviews), disseminated or utilized in any form or by any means, electronic or mechanical, including photocopying, recording, or in any information storage and retrieval system, or the Internet/World Wide Web without written permission from the author or publisher.

Printed in the United States of America
First Edition Printing

Cover Photos by Rob B. Dutton

Design by
Arbor Services, Inc.
http://www.arborservices.co/

Letting Go...Holding On - Surrendering to Life As It Is
Anne Lesley Lanier

ISBN: 978-0-692-16664-2
LCCN: 2018909062
1. Title 2. Author 3. Poetry

Letting Go... Holding On:

Surrendering to Life As It Is

Anne L. Lanier

DEDICATION

For my friend Kath, one who has laughed with me, cried with me, and stayed with me in the brokenness and the healing . . . One who trusted that I had courage to live and to live strong. One who always has the right words, the right touch—one who has the "gentle effect."

With gratitude always to Melissa and Michael and all they gift to my life

Always remembering Chris . . .
December 25, 1988 – August 4, 2013
"I see you"

"Strength does not come from physical capacity, it comes from an indomitable will."

---Gandhi

OTHER BOOKS BY ANNE

Walking the Path of Grief
Like a Rose
When Time Stands Still
In the Same Boat
Just Thinking
Sitting with the Mountain and a Dog Named Bear
Beginning Again . . .
Opening Doors
Stepping Stones
Always Beginning Again . . .
Reaching for the Light
Finding a New Way Home . . .

Table of Contents

Dedication	iv	That Is Life	41
Connecting to Life	1	Showing Up	42
Once Upon a Time	2	The Presence of Absence	43
Life Is Letting Go	3	Held with Sadness	44
The Light Will Come	4	Making It Through	45
It All Matters	5	Get Up Again	46
Being	6	What Do You See	47
We Wait	7	No Separation	48
A Good-bye to My Dad	8	Connection . . . or Not . . .	49
Grace	9	Learning to Be Strong	50
To Be Found	10	Beauty Surrounds Us	51
Not Alone	11	Everyone Matters	53
A Bigger Picture	12	To Believe	54
Things As They Are	13	Life Is Learning	55
Letting Go	14	Trust	56
The Story Is Already Told	16	Just Surrender	57
The Hardest of Places	17	To Surrender	58
Time Stands Still	18	One with Love	59
Some Days	19	A Kind of Dying	60
It Matters	20	Hope in Hopelessness	61
Journeying Together	21	Healing through Surrender	62
To Grow Hope	22	The Space Between	63
Just Wandering	23	The In-Between Time	64
When Someone Sees	24	Always Moving	65
Each Piece Belongs	25	Now	66
To Hold onto Life	26	Beginnings	67
And Still, I Cry	27	Dear One	68
Follow	28	A New Path	69
Walls	29	Doorways	70
Every Once in a While	31	Opening the Door to Healing	71
Time	32	The Only Answer	72
To Let Fear Go	33	What Will Be	73
The Way to Healing	34	Learning to Let It Go	74
There Is Beauty	35	On Bravery	75
Words That Will Not Come	36	The Difference to Know	76
Gentle Effect	37	11 Days to Coming Home	77
To Live Strong	38	Being Lost . . . Being Found	79
Beauty	39	A Little at a Time	80
Fair Enough	40	I Wish We Could Remember	81

With Each Step	82	Where the Healing Begins	112
Loving, Learning, Working	83	When Courage Meets Fear	113
Another Letting Go	84	Being with Time	114
After Awhile	85	We Give What We Have	115
Love All Around	86	By Example	116
Who We Are	87	Words	117
Walk with What Is Broken	88	Winter in the Spring	118
Becoming Alive	89	We Find Our Way	119
Allowing Life	90	The Question with No Answer	120
We Are One	91	Let the Truth In	121
Something Called Grace	92	Moments in Time	122
Moments of Wonder	93	Something to Hold Onto	123
Nothing to Hold Onto	94	Letting Go of Questions	124
What Is Enough	95	No Regrets When We Choose Love	125
Beauty in Courage	96	Be Brave Enough	126
This Story	97	No Loopholes	127
Words of the Heart	98	A Way to Peace	128
You Are . . . You Belong	99	Surrender to the Truth	129
Letting the Truth In	100	Up to Us	130
Being Ordinary	101	There Is Always Good	131
Lost Moments	102	A Backpack of Rocks	132
A Question	103	An Act of Courage	133
Leaving	104	Day by Day	134
Sometimes	105	Always	135
It All Matters II	106	When Fear Slips In	136
What Is Silence?	107	We Are Never Alone	137
In the End	108	Another Day	138
Being Lost	109	The Truth	139
To Trust	110	About the Arthur:	140
Looking for Rainbows	111		

Connecting to Life

There are times in our lives
When we need
Someone, something
To connect us to life
To keep reminding us
There is something bigger than us
Something at work in the Universe
That will someday
Bring all the pieces into place
Reveal a deeper mystery
A destiny
A reason
For everything that has happened
For everything that will happen
That knows we are all where we are meant to be
Learning
Living
Connecting
Connecting to life

Once Upon a Time

When someone dies
Someone you were once connected to
Someone who was your world once upon a time
Until they left
Because
Well, you didn't fit into their story anymore
There is this deep sadness that seeps in
A sadness that
Even though
Your stories were always connected
You lived your lives as if you didn't know
Not letting love in
Not letting love grow
Not letting love connect you
To be who you were meant to be
And you were meant to be
Together
Once upon a time
And always

Life Is Letting Go

It seems to be a truth
That life is about letting go
Surrendering to what is
And to what is not
Because when you surrender
You stop fighting against life
And start going with the flow
And when you are going with the flow
You can breathe
You can let things be
You can be
Just be
Be flowing
Be gentle
Be with life
Even though
You are letting it go

The Light Will Come

Last night
I forgot
Forgot that when the waves come
That they will go back
They'll go back where they came from
And leave you to catch your breath again
But in the forgetting
It becomes very dark
There is that voice
The one that asks why
And still waits for the answer
The one that whispers no one cares
And still waits for the phone to ring
The one that screams into the darkness
And still waits for the light
The answer does not come
The phone does not ring
But the light comes
The light comes
And I will try to remember that next time
For surely there will be a next time
And just as surely
The light will come

It All Matters

There are times
When it seems nothing matters
And that voice inside
Says what's the point?
No matter what
There is pain
There is hurt
There is disappointment
But then
There is another voice
That says
Look!
Don't you see?
Everything matters
How you live your life
How you live this day
This minute
Don't be fooled
By the things that hurt
The things that disappoint
For there is a reason
And it matters
It all matters

Being

Sometimes
I wonder
Why I bother
Why tend to the flowers
Why look others in the eyes
Why listen
Why watch and wait
Why create beauty
Why bother
But then
I know it matters
It has to matter
That someone cares
That someone tends to the little things
And that we tend to each other
Watching
Noticing
Seeing
Being present
Being
Just being

We Wait

My dad died last night
A man I didn't really know
He left us behind many years ago
Leaving us to live his life somewhere else, with someone else
And the years went by
Years of wondering
When would he return?
But it was not to be
He made his choice
To stay away
And so I wonder
Was it worth it?
All the lost years
All the lost time
Did he know we waited for him?
Does he know?
We wait still
Does he know?
We will always wait for him

A Good-bye to My Dad

I am so sorry that you are gone
And I didn't get to say good-bye
Good-bye to you
Good-bye to all that was lost
The years of separation
You never knowing my kids
You not being in my life
Please know I love you anyway
For you will always be my dad
I have been missing you all my life
And so now
With this final good-bye
All I can say
Is
May you know peace
May you know you are loved
May you know
I have always missed you
Miss you still
Will always miss you

Grace

When someone leaves
And the heartbreak is palpable
Yet what you feel
Along with the pain and tears
Is gratitude
Gratitude for who they have been in your life
Gratitude for their words, their guidance, their teaching, their light
Then surely
This is love
And surely
There is hope
For letting go
And for connection to still be there
For grace
Surely . . . somehow
There is grace

To Be Found

There are times
When feeling lost
Or seeing that you are lost
Rudderless perhaps
And without direction
Is a good thing
A very good thing
Because then
And only then
Can you begin again
Can you begin to find your way
And to be found
And so
Maybe
To get lost
Is the beginning of being found

Not Alone

When I can remember
I try to look through eyes of compassion
And for me
Those eyes
See everyone as broken in some way
Broken in a way
That says we are not alone
We are all broken
We each have hurting places
Places where the two-year-old, the eight-year-old,
　　the ten-year-old waits
Waits and watches for the connection
That connecting point
That says we are alike
We are one
We are not alone

A Bigger Picture

If we could remember
There is a bigger picture
There is always a bigger picture
Where all the pieces come together
Where what I do
And what you do
Comes together
To make a difference
To make the bigger picture
So that
Everything we do
Or don't do
Matters
It all matters
It all has a place in the picture
The picture of our lives

Things As They Are

Do we ever see things as they are?
Is that ever possible?
With all the different ways to see
With all the stories we tell
Ourselves
And others
How could there ever be
"Things as they are"
Because, of course,
You only let me see
What you want me to see
And I only let you see
What I want you to see
So that
Things as they are
Is a moving target
Always changing
Never really as they are
And yet
At the same time
It is what it is
Both are true
Both are true

Letting Go

In meditation
We are taught to focus on the breath
And this morning
As I sat breathing in, breathing out
It suddenly came to me
What is life
If not learning to let go?
It is there
In the breath
Breathing in, breathing out
In the waters
In the ebb and in the flow
In all of life
The closed bud opens, blooms, and fades
The womb opens
A new life begins
Breathing in, breathing out
Leaves flutter to the ground
The seasons change
The sun rises, the sun sets
The moon rises,
The moon sets
The clouds open, the rains fall
Breathing in, breathing out
The heart opens, love comes in, love returns
We learn, we grow, we change

We laugh, we cry
We hold on, we let go
We surrender
Letting go
Life goes on
Breathing in, breathing out

The Story Is Already Told

I've been trying to catch up with myself lately
Trying to put words to the blank pages before me
And what I am finding is
The words are already written
The story is already told
The words just have to find their way to the blank page
We just have to keep turning the page
Moving toward the next chapter
It may take a little while
To find the right words
To put them in the right order
Not unlike putting a puzzle together
There is a place for each piece
For each word
They just have to find their way to the blank page
The story is already told

The Hardest of Places

There are some things in life that break your heart
There are some things that threaten your existence
They are hard
They shake the ground you stand on
Cracking your foundation
And sometimes
Through those hardest of places,
You find yourself.
The softest of love comes through
And holds on
Holds on and won't let go
And it brings grace and healing
A grace that brings new life
New life that comes from the ashes
Just like the phoenix rising
You find yourself
And you begin again
You learn to live
With the heart broken open
With arms wide open
You learn to live in the ebb and flow
You learn to be hurting and healing

Time Stands Still

There are some days
When time stands still
And when these days come around
Maybe the best we can do
Is stay with them
Wait
While the memories come
And the memories go
Let the day take us
Wherever it will take us
Let love hold us
Let the heart be filled
With all that is good
With all that is full of wonder
Let love in
Let gratitude in
Let life in
And then
Watch
As time begins to move again
Ever so gently
Covered with the softness of good-bye again
Covered with the knowing
That the gift of time
Watches and waits with us
The gift of time waits for us
Even as
Life goes on

Some Days

Some days
I just want to be alone
Watching
As the birds come and go
Finding the feeder outside the window
As the branches sway in the breeze
As leaves flutter to the ground
And the shadows dance with the light
Listening
As the breath comes and goes
As the sounds of silence
Fill the house, the room, my heart
So that I can
Perhaps
Be with what is
And still be with peace
Be in wonder of this life
Even with its angst and its pain
Be with all of it
And be in love
With life
As it is
As it always has been
As it always will be

It Matters

One of my neighbors
Just eight years old
Came running down the sidewalk today
Calling to me
Did you find the flower?
The one in the mailbox?
She was so excited
Saying she left it there for me
I had been doing such good work she said
And then she hugged me
An eight-year-old hug
Bubbling over with her gifts
Of goodness
Of kindness
Bubbling over with her truth
That love was all around
That love was in a flower
A flower placed carefully in the mailbox
A flower that says
What you do matters
What each of us does matters
It all matters

Journeying Together

It has been said
It is hard to find your way
In the dark
And that is why
We need each other
We need to journey together
At least, most of the time
Sometimes one shines the light
And sometimes another
We carry each other
Hold each other
Guide each other
Teach each other
And though there are times
When we need to reflect on our own
We need each other
Need to know we are not alone
We need to walk together
To sit together
To stand together
To lean on each other
To love each other
To let love be ever present

To Grow Hope

The work of grief
Though it is hard work
Is not meant to complicate life
But rather
To heal life
And so
If we could surrender to it
Let ourselves be with the process
And have it take us
Then
There would come a day
When we could let go of what has hurt us
And use it
To give us strength and courage
To give us gentleness and compassion
That we could then give away
And we could use
To grow hope and light and peace

Just Wandering

Sometimes
There are things
That make time stand still
They may last only a moment
But they stay with you
Long after the moment has passed
And today
There was such a moment
A mother deer and her two babies appeared on the path I walked
I stopped and waited
Watching
As they wandered down the path
And it struck me in that moment
That as I wandered down that same path
We were one in that moment of time
Four beings
Just wandering
Living
Just living
Being
Just being

When Someone Sees

Someone wrote to me
"I can't begin to know your pain"
And then she said
"I hope the gift of your quiet, patient presence
That you give to others . . .
Brings you some comfort . . ."
And with those words
I knew my soul had been seen
That my way of being in this world
Had been understood somehow
And being awakened with such gentleness
The depth of my being stirred
Opened and softened
My whole world became soft
Became light
And the tears came
Tears of wonder
Tears of strength and courage
Tears of knowing
Knowing that what we do
What we do with our pain
How we hold it
How we use it to hold others
It matters
In this life
In this moment . . . it matters

Each Piece Belongs

A sense of belonging
It seems
Is one key to a life of peace and hope
To feel welcome
To know you belong
That you are loved
That you are connected
Connected and one with all
That your piece of the puzzle
Has a place
That it fits
That it matters
That it completes the bigger picture
And to know that all are connected
That each piece matters
Each piece belongs
To become whole
We need each and every piece
Each and every one
To be included
To complete the picture
To find our place
To bring wholeness
To create a world at peace

To Hold onto Life

I think I finally understand
How to find a place called acceptance
When something heartbreaking has happened
The heart will always be broken
No matter what the "experts" say
But there is a shift that happens
So that
Just as with an earthquake
Where the ground has shifted
The foundation has been shaken
And it can seem as if all is lost
Gradually
There is a settling that happens
You can begin to rebuild
And in the rebuilding
You let go of things that weigh you down, that hold you down
But you hold onto the things that give you life
As it is
You hold on
To life

And Still, I Cry

There are no words for some things
The feelings seem too deep
The heartbreak too much
And still
Life is good
And that is even harder sometimes
To put into words
Because
Still
I cry
There is love and beauty all around
There is gratitude
There is learning, changing, growing
There is healing
Life is good
No matter what
And still
I cry
For the love that is lost
For all that will never be
For the lives that will never be
For the lives that will never be the same
I cry
Even knowing life is good
Allowing it all
Surrendering
Still
I cry

Follow

You know how people say
If something keeps coming to you
Whether it is a thought, a dream, an idea
It is a nudge from the Universe
So listen
It has something to tell you
And if the Universe has something to say
It must be pretty important
For you
For your life
Maybe for the rest of your life
So they say
Don't wait too long
Watch and listen
But then
Follow
For it is your heart and soul
Waiting for you

Walls

It is said
That you cannot run out of love
That the more you give
The more you get
So why is it so hard
To be open and vulnerable
To love
Without reservation
Without resistance
What happens that we build walls
That we don't let others in
That we don't give love
Without expectations
And then there are the real walls that come to be
Built to separate and isolate
Built to protect
But protect who?
From what?
For love?
These walls we build
Inside and out
They are fear
They need to come down and they will
They will come down
When we learn to love
Really love

Without conditions
When we learn to forgive and be real
When there is no more room for hate
No more room for separation

Every Once in a While

Every once in a while
We catch someone's eye
We pause
And capture a moment in time
See something
Something that comes from the soul
And for that moment
If we choose
We see each other
Really see each other
See what has no words
But says everything
Lets us know
The depth of love
Sometimes the love that is there
Sometimes the love that is needed

Time

Time is a curious thing
Sometimes it seems to move so quickly
Sometimes it seems to move so slowly
Sometimes it seems to stand still
Sometimes timing is everything
Sometimes timing is nothing at all
And the funny thing is
Time is nothing
And time is everything
It is a clock on the wall
A number on the phone, on a watch, on a scoreboard
And it is the constant movement of the past
Into the present
Into the future
The constant movement from here to there
From thought, to word, to experience
From baby steps, to hope, to healing
It is nothing at all, it is everything
Time is love
Love to be lost or found
To be taken or to be given
Time is what it is
Time is what we make of it

To Let Fear Go

Fear blocks us from love sometimes
Fear of not being enough
Fear of not knowing enough
Fear of "the other"
Maybe fear of change
Maybe fear of being judged
Or maybe it is judging
But what is the worst that could happen
If you reach out
If you open your heart
If you keep putting one foot in front of the other
If you show up
Maybe you don't get to know someone you didn't know
Don't get to experience what you haven't experienced
Don't get to go where you haven't been
So maybe
Just maybe it would be okay
To let go of fear
And in the letting go
We could let love in
Get to know someone we didn't know
Get to experience something we haven't
Get to go somewhere we haven't been
Get to learn and grow and change
Get to live without fear

The Way to Healing

There are times in our lives
When we have to slow down
Maybe even stop and wait
Wait and watch as leaves flutter to the ground
Wait and watch as the winds blow
As the flowers begin to bloom
As the sun rises
And the sun sets
Be with the silence
Be with what darkness there may be
Knowing, time keeps moving
And yet
It is in the waiting and watching
It is in the silence and the darkness
That we can begin to see the light
Begin to find our way
Our way to healing
Our way to acceptance

There Is Beauty

There are some things
That are beautiful
In their own way
Not the way you would have wanted
But when people gather
In love
To remember
To hold each other up
To be together
There is beauty
In heartbreak
And sorrow
And loss
There is beauty
There is gratitude
There is wonder
In the telling of stories
In the laughter
In the connections made
In the photographs
The memories
The tears
There is beauty
In its own way
But gosh
Not the way you would have wanted . . . *not the way you would have wanted*

Words That Will Not Come

Some nights are so very long
And sometimes they come in the middle of the day
Waves of pain can feel unbearable
And there are no words
That feel like enough
To make what is felt at the core of your being
Make it feel understood
So that
You feel heard, feel seen, feel consoled
But
It is said
That the sun will always rise
That there will be light again
Light and love enough
So that
The words that will not come
Can be laid to rest somehow
And someday
Let go
Let go with the waves

Gentle Effect

You know how when you send a text
You can send it with gentle effect
And the message is sent with a certain slowness
Gets bigger, then smaller
Like taking a big breath and letting it go . . . slowly
Like a sigh really
And my friend said to me,
"Give yourself gentle effect"
Telling me
To hold my fear and apprehension
With gentleness
So that
It doesn't get too big
But it is acknowledged
And then it becomes smaller
Being held with gentle effect
And then
And then
There is room for excitement and anticipation
For hope and love
Room for holding it all
With gentle effect

To Live Strong

Sometimes
You just need one someone
To have faith for you
When you have lost yours
To hold onto hope for you
When what you feel is despair
To believe in love
When you feel the sting of rejection
And just one someone
To trust
To trust that you have courage
Courage to live
And to live strong
Living with faith in faith
Hope in hope
Believing in love
And trusting in courage
The courage to live strong

Beauty

There is beauty in the imperfection
Sometimes, it is even more beautiful
Than perfection itself
Because
Perfection can seem sterile, tense, harsh
It can be without warmth and softness
But in imperfection
Is what is real
There are the bumps and bruises
The broken places and the wrinkles
The wounds and the scars
All that is real
All that is imperfect
All that makes us vulnerable
Makes us strong as well
Makes us real
Makes us perfect
Makes us beautiful

Fair Enough

It is said
That life is not fair
And I wonder
Is that even something to grasp for
Because
Life is not fair
It never has been
It never will be
Even with all the checks and balances
For some
For most of us
There will be times
When life is not fair
And yet
There is enough
That is good and healing and wonder-full
And for that
There is gratitude
Somehow
Makes it fair enough
Makes it fair enough

That Is Life

As I was bent down in the garden
Someone walking by said
I'm impressed you can still get down
And my reply came quickly
It's even better that I can still get up
And there was laughter
And agreement
But then I thought
That is life
You go down
You are knocked down
And you get up
Somehow
To keep going
You have to find a way
To get up
Even if it is just in your mind
You get up
You find a reason
A purpose
To keep going
Until the next time you are down
And you do it again
You get up
You keep going

Showing Up

It is said that showing up matters
Matters for the whole
And it is true
If I come with my 20% that I have to give
And you come with your 60%
And we connect
Because we showed up
Then maybe
Just maybe
There will be some healing
And my 20% will become 30
Your 60% will become 70
And together
We make another 100%
And showing up
Has made us whole
Showing up
Has made a difference
Has been the difference

The Presence of Absence

There are times
When the presence
Of someone's absence
Is even bigger than their presence
Because they are no longer here
They are always here
There seem to be reminders
No matter where you go
And there are signs
Signs that they are not here
And the ache inside
From the presence of their absence
Is something so indescribable
And yet so real
Is something that has no words
And yet
It is with you always
Just there
Waiting and watching
So that
You see with different eyes
You feel with a different heart
You hear and touch with a different knowing
And you
You are a different kind of presence

Held with Sadness

It's hard to accept
That for the rest of one's life
Every happy moment
No matter how filled with joy
Will always be held with sadness
Because someone who should have been here
Is gone
Someone who was supposed to be a part of these moments
Is lost
And it will never be okay
There will never be just happiness
Ever
Because there is a hole in the middle of things
Because of the heartbreak
Because there will always be the thought
He should have been here

Making It Through

There are some people
Or maybe it is each of us
At some times
We have opportunities to be that person
The one who makes us believe
We're gonna make it through this
No matter what "this" is
And I don't know how it happens
But if we could remind each other of that
If we could believe that . . .
That we can make it through
If we could remember that
Be reminded
That all we have to do
Is keep getting up
Keep putting one foot in front of the other
Keep believing
You will make it through
You will make it through

Get Up Again

There are so many lessons to learn
In this life
Lessons from looking within
Lessons from looking without
And it seems
The lesson that keeps coming around
Is when you fall down
When you are knocked down
When you fail
When you make a wrong decision
Don't stop there
At least
Not for long
Get up
Again and again and again
Get up
Rest if you have to
Need to
But get up
Keep going
Live the life you are given
Live it
Completely
Get up again

What Do You See

What do you see
When you see with different eyes
When you see how fleeting life is
And how little time we have
Do you see how beautiful everything is
And how broken?
Do you see
That all that matters
And that brings healing to this hurting world
Is how well we love
How much we open
How much we connect
How far we can see
That we are all one
Do you see
Can you see
What do you see
Can you say
To the person next to you
I see you

No Separation

I watched yesterday
As three sisters and their brother
Sat at the bedside
Where their mother lay dying
Trying so hard to connect
The wanting that was in each heart
And the picture, the vision that came
Seemed so real, so true
It seemed the mother lay on one side of an unseen window
One that was beginning to close
The children—though grown up
Clamored at the window
There was laughter and conversation
And the window was open just then
So they could touch each other
Hear each other
See each other clearly
And I wondered
Would the window stay open long enough
For the love and concern in their hearts
To become one
To be seen
So that
When the window closed
They would have the connection they longed for
And there would be no separation

Connection . . . or Not . . .

Connection can be such a fleeting thing
Or at least, so it seems
When there is an openness for a moment
And then just as quickly
You see the shadow pass across the eyes
Feel the energy begin to change
And the conversation changes too
It becomes about all the reasons why
Why you can't be present
It becomes about next time
Maybe
It becomes about how busy you are
How sorry you are
That it didn't work out this time
How very sorry you are
But next time
For sure
And thank you
Thank you for understanding
Thank you for your flexibility
And there you are
With that familiar ache inside
Because it didn't work out
This time

Learning to Be Strong

It is true no one's life is perfect
We all hit bumps in the road
There will always be roadblocks
And things to work out
And maybe that's what life is all about
Facing adversity
Falling down
Getting up
Learning to persevere
To be resilient
To be strong
And as you learn
As you stay with life
You find love and hope
You find light and happiness
You find
The beauty of what is imperfect
You find what is perfect
And it is life
Just as it is
Bumps and roadblocks
Falling down and getting up
Learning
To be strong

Beauty Surrounds Us

It is hard sometimes
To remember all the beauty
The beauty that surrounds us every moment
The sun, the trees, the grass
The rocks, the sand, the water
And the majesty—oh! The majesty
Of oceans and mountains and forests
And the little tiny things
Ladybugs, butterflies, bees, and ants
And then the things we cannot touch
Music, love, compassion
So much beauty surrounding us
And maybe
There is some beauty in the brokenness, too
The gifts that come from our wounds
The calm, the softness, the peace
The seeing and hearing what is truly there
But, oh
The price we pay
Sometimes it hides the beauty
Sometimes it covers the light
Making it hard to find our way back
Making it hard to remember
There is so much beauty
Beauty that saves us in the end
Reminds us to be grateful

For what is left
For what stays
For what surrounds us
For what holds us
Even when we cannot remember
Cannot remember
All the beauty
That surrounds us

Everyone Matters

There is this tenderness within
Growing in the darkness like moss growing over a rock
It is covering my heart and mind
My eyes and ears
So that
When looking out at the world
There is a softness
A longing for peace and love and hope
There is this way of seeing
Seeing the pain that is all around
Seeing the pain that is all around
And holding it
With tenderness
So that
There are connections made
There is understanding
There is peace and love and hope
And yet
There is still longing
Longing to be seen and heard and held with care
Longing to matter
And maybe
That is what we all long for
To feel that we matter
Even when we know
Everyone matters

To Believe

If everyone matters
And we do
Everyone matters
Everyone is needed in this mixed-up world
How can it be
That so many struggle to know it
To feel it
To embrace it
To embrace it and the possibilities that come
When you know you matter
That you make a difference
And when you know
When you believe
Then
You become one with all that is
Then
Your life is peace

Life Is Learning

In some ways
Life is learning to be
To be with the disappointments
The challenges
The roadblocks
The cutoffs and the storms
Learning to be
With what is not to be
And moving beyond
To what is to be
To what is possible
And finding, learning
That what is beyond the challenge
The roadblock
The cutoff and the storm
Is what you've been waiting for
Is what you need
To be
Who you are meant to be

Trust

If you trust yourself
That's all you really need
To listen to your heart
Follow what it tells you
And then
Even if it seems to not work out
It's okay
Because you trusted yourself
And when you trust yourself
It's not about whether it works out
It's about knowing you followed your heart
And the pieces will fall into place
It will be all right
And you will learn
Through the heart
And that journey is taken
Learning who you are
Learning what you need
To find your way home

Just Surrender

There are times it seems
When all that's left to do
Is
To surrender
Like a leaf floating to the earth
Like a cloud drifting across the sky
Like a ripple moving across the water
Just surrender
To what is
To what is seen
And what is unseen
And then just believe
Believe that it will all work out in the end
There is a reason why
And all there is to do
Is surrender

To Surrender

To get to a place of surrender
Is a messy business
Because before you get there
There is a deep journey
A journey to the deepest parts of who you are
Where there is darkness
Pain and tears
So many tears
Where there is denial and bargaining
More pain
More tears
A heaviness and aching inside
That feels like it could smother you
Feels like it will not let you go
The depth of the journey
Is impossible to imagine
Sometimes feels impossible to travel
But travel it you must
For life is worth every step
Love is worth every tear
Surrender is worth the journey
The journey to become like a leaf
Floating to the earth
To become like the breath
Floating on the air

One with Love

They say
The way to happiness
Is to keep looking forward
To not look back
But sometimes
What is left behind
What is missing
Is what you see and feel
Even as you look forward
Even as you seek happiness
And so it seems
Moving forward, finding happiness
Is not about forgetting
But rather
Is about finding ways
To bring the memories with you
Move them forward as well
So that
You are full
Full with all the love you have known
And ready to be filled with all the love you will know
Past, present, and future
All together
All of it making you . . . you
Making you . . . love
Making you one . . . with love

A Kind of Dying

Grief
I've come to learn
Is a kind of dying
As you fight
To hold on tight
And struggle to let go
You have to learn
To not fight the waves of despair
And at the same time
To let the struggle go
The struggle to make sense of it
The struggle to surrender
The struggle to accept your life
Just as it is
With the ache of loss ever present
With the holding on
With the letting go
To accept
This is a kind of dying
This is the way of life

Hope in Hopelessness

There are times
When you feel such hopelessness
And it's hard to know
What to do next
It's hard to even think about moving forward
And there are those
Who try to tell you
It is never hopeless
But yes
Yes, sometimes it is
And the thing is
In the face of hopelessness
There is still something to learn
There are still ways to grow
You just have to give yourself the gift of time
Give yourself time to breathe
And there will be
Hope
In the hopelessness

Healing through Surrender

Sometimes
When something is happening to us
Within us
Around us
The only choice we have
Is to surrender to it
Let it happen
Let it teach us
Grow in us
As it will
For as long as it will
Guide us
To a new understanding
A new peace
Guide us
To healing
Healing through surrender

The Space Between

When you've lost someone close to you
It is true what they say
That you feel them
In the spaces between things
In the times they should be there
In the jacket they used to wear
In the pictures
Your memory brings them back
And you feel them
Feel them in the spaces
And long for them to come home
To fill in the spaces
Because that's where they should be
That's where they belong
They should be there
They should be here
In the space between

The In-Between Time

Sometimes
Life seems to stand still
And you just have to cry
And if you're trying not to cry
Nothing works
And you just have to let it go
And it's always such a surprise
That once you cry
Once the tears have fallen down your cheeks
Been released
Been let go
Then
Somehow
You can breathe again
And then
You can
Not cry
Because it is done
Until the next time
But for now
There is the in-between time
When life goes on

Always Moving

Some days, my love
I still think—
How can I get through this day?
It hurts too much
The pain of losing you
I cry
I breathe
I hold on to what is here
And somehow
I get through the day
I can see all that is good again
All that I am grateful for
And life keeps moving forward
We keep moving forward
Because
I guess
No matter what
We are always moving
We just have to stay
Stay with the movement
Stay with all of life
The love, the loss
The pain, the gratitude

Now

Today
I was walking with my dog
Early in the morning
In a softly falling snow
It was so quiet
Barely light enough to see
Christmas lights shining from porches
The snow just covering the landscape
It felt so very peaceful
We walked around the block a second time
Our footprints still visible in the snow
But covered completely in places
And I thought
This is life
We leave a mark here and there
A mark that says we were here
And then
We are gone, it is gone
And soon enough there is no sign
That we were here at all
At least no sign that anyone truly sees as us
And so
Now is the time to walk with intention
Now is the time to be here
Now is the time
Be here now

Beginnings

Sometimes
It feels like life is slipping by
And yet
Other times
It feels like life is just beginning
That I'm just beginning to understand
That to love and accept others
I must love and accept myself
To trust others
I must trust myself
To believe in others
I must believe in myself
To live my life fully
I must be here now
Staying in the present moment
Appreciating it for what it is
Knowing there is pain
And there is beauty
There is death
There is life
There are endings
And there are beginnings
Always, always
There are beginnings

Dear One

There is someone I know
Who calls me "dear one"
And truth be known
I think she calls everyone "dear one"
But still
To be called "dear one"
With such tenderness
With such gentleness
Surrounding me as it does
With kindness, hope, and love
It feels like a warm blanket on a cold night
Or the soft glow of candlelight in the darkness
It is grace
To be called "dear one"
It is grace
To be someone's dear one

A New Path

I walked around the block today
Leaving footprints in the snow
And the second time I walked
Try as I might
My steps would not fall in the same places
Or in the same way for more than a step or two
And it made me think
We are always on a new path
For we have changed
If only a tiny bit
Each time we take a step
Something bigger is guiding our steps perhaps
So that
They are never the same
They are always leading us
On a new path
A path that leads us home
Leads us where we need to go

Doorways

I've been thinking a lot about doorways lately
And how
It is always our choice
Which doors to open
But then again
It seems there is some destiny as well
So how do you choose
Is it just the one in front of you
Or is there one you need to find
You have the key to the right one for you
Perhaps
And that is the one that will open with ease
That is the one that you can walk through without stumbling
It is the one
That when you open it
And step across the threshold
Everything on the other side
Says, "Welcome home, welcome home."
And so you stay
Until you see the next doorway
And everything about it
Says come
Come and see
See what waits for you

Opening the Door to Healing

Sometimes
It feels like you are on a threshold
Something in your life
Is changing
Something is calling to you
Wanting you to be who you are
Wanting you to know
You are enough
Just as you are
But first
You have to open the door to healing
Remember who you are
Let that person free
And then
You learn to be
The you
You were meant to be

The Only Answer

Opening to love
You would think it was the easiest thing in this world
But for some
It is the biggest challenge of all
There are so many reasons not to trust
All the disappointments and broken promises that have come before
The abandonment
The cutoffs
And yet
Love is the answer
Opening to love is the question
The question we must all face
And if we are to let go
If we are to learn and grow
If we are to let life in
The only answer
Is yes
The only answer is to open the door to love

What Will Be

It's hard sometimes
To open the heart to what will be
Fear of the unknown
Fear of not being enough
Of not being worthy
All these fears
Keep the heart closed
And locked
And the key, I think
To opening that lock
To opening the heart
Is trust
Trust that there is love and light
Trust that there will be what we need
That we will be what is needed
And we will be
If we trust
If we show up
Just as we are
To find what will be

Learning to Let It Go

Learning to go with the flow
Is not really a fluid process
There are stops and starts
There are blocks and forgetting
We need reminders
All the time
To not get stuck
To not let hurt and disappointment
Block our way to going with the flow
So that
When things happen
That are painful or disappointing
When words spoken are hard and jagged
We forget to let it wash over us
We forget
But then a reminder will come
Something simple usually
Soft words
A soft touch
Soft eyes
And then, maybe
You are learning to go with the flow once more
You are learning to let it go

On Bravery

Someone said last night
There can be no bravery
Without fear
And that was so important to hear
That breaking through the fear
Is where we find what is possible
And what is possible
Is to find out
Who we are
And that is the question to ask
When stepping out into the world
Or even when exploring our inner world
Who am I?
For that is where we find out . . .
On the other side of fear
On the other side of being brave
That is who we are

The Difference to Know

Someone much wiser than I
Said to know there is a difference
Between fear and danger
And that is so important
Because most of the time
We are telling ourselves a story
The fear or the danger
Is in our minds
Not even real
And what a difference it would make
What a different way to live
Knowing what is real
Staying with what is real
Letting go of fear
Or, at least, working through it
To find no danger there

11 Days to Coming Home

I went on a journey recently
11 days of being grounded in Mother Earth
11 days of watching for rainbows
Of doorways
And crossing bridges
There were ruins to explore
And pathways and steps to climb
And with every step
My life began to change
My heart began to open
And though there is still sadness
There is so much light
The light of being guided with so much love and care
The light of hearing "this one is strong, this one has wisdom"
The light of seeing hearts open
Of seeing the ruins of our inner worlds begin to heal and come to life
And for me, the brightest light of all
A young boy
Taking my hands
And gifting me with words from his heart to mine
"I will be your son, you will be my mother"
11 days of walking and sometimes pausing together
11 days of healing
11 days to be connected
Forever

And with every rainbow I see
I will remember
Walkers on a path
Hearts opening
Hearts softening and healing
Hearts saying, "I see you"
Hearts coming home

Being Lost . . . Being Found

There is a new perspective to learn
On nearly everything
And one I am most grateful for
Is a new way of being lost
For being lost can be
A most distressing place to be
But can you imagine
"Being lost in excitement?"
Or being lost "in the wonder of it all?"
For life is full of excitement and wonder
Such wonder
So that
Being lost in that way
There is expectation, not fear
There is growth, not paralysis
There is
Wonder
There is
Peace and love
There is being found

A Little at a Time

Healing is a lifelong journey
One that requires remembering
Remembering what has hurt you
And, letting it go
Letting the pain go
A little at a time
Or, at least, letting go when it is time
And letting it go
Means your heart opens
A little bit more
Each time you surrender
Love and light come in
Doors open for moments of joy
Making room for you to breathe
Making room for healing
A little at a time

I Wish We Could Remember

Life goes on
I wish we could remember that
On those dark nights
On those days
When nothing seems to work
And it seems too hard
Or it feels overwhelming
Life goes on
When the loneliness feels suffocating
Or the pain too deep
I wish we could remember
That life goes on
Winter becomes spring
Rain becomes blue skies
The darkest night becomes the day
The sun will always shine again
Buds will come
Flowers will bloom
Trees will grow
Life goes on
I wish we could remember that
On those dark nights
That life goes on

With Each Step

There is a meditation
Where you say
"I am here" with one step
And "I am home" with the next
And you find
As you walk
That with each step
You are here
You are home
And really
That is where the path is
It is here
And that is where the path goes
It goes home

Loving, Learning, Working

There is a philosophy of life
A teaching
That tells us to live life well
There must be balance
The balance
Of loving
Of learning
Of working
And to live life this way
You open to love and hope
You learn to let go of pain and doubt
You learn to hold on to what is left
To what is good
And then life will flow
There will be surrendering
And there will be signs
There will be beauty even in heartbreak
There will be healing
There will be peace

Another Letting Go

There is always another letting go
When you have lost someone dear
A wave of grief will come
When you lose something connected to them
But then
If you are lucky
Someone else is standing there
Offering you a gift
A gift from their heart to yours
And if you have done the work of letting go
Then you can receive this gift
With your broken heart
Your broken heart
That is still letting go
Still healing
Opening to what is here
Opening to what will be

After Awhile

After awhile
You come to understand
That surrendering, is being strong
That letting go, is holding on
And so,
You surrender to what is
You hold on to what is left
And you give yourself freedom
Freedom to live your life
Even when your heart is broken
Freedom to feel love and joy again
Even if through the filter of sadness
You begin to let life flow
Flow through you
Flow around you
You open your arms
Open your hands
You open to what is
You open your heart
And then you will find
Life is a gift
There you will know
Life goes on

Love All Around

I was on a pilgrimage recently
Hiking in the mountains of Peru
And maybe it was the thin air
But I saw a man in the mountain
And he looked on me with such kindness
Such compassion
And the words he spoke
"I see you" he said . . . "I see you"
And there it was
What we all long for
To be seen
To be heard
To be understood
And there it was
Such love and caring all around
Holding us
Protecting us
Seeing us

Who We Are

We are always asking ourselves
Who am I
Now
Now that this has happened
Now that that has happened
And it does change
With each experience
With each passing day
But maybe the spirit within that we carry
Stays the same
And that is who we truly are
That is what we bring to this life
And that is what we leave behind
That is what stays
It is our true nature that is remembered
And that is who we are

Walk with What Is Broken

There are many things to learn in this life
Many doorways to cross
And one of the things
You must do
Is stand up again
When you have been broken
When your heart is in a million pieces on the floor
Know you are still strong
You can still be brave
You must give shelter to what is
Walk with what is broken
Let what is broken in you
Gently melt into you
Become a part of you
And then you walk as one
The broken and the whole
And that is what makes us real in this life
That is what makes everything real
And when we are real
There is love
All around
There is love

Becoming Alive

There are times
We are called to go on a pilgrimage
Not necessarily hiking winding paths
Or traveling to faraway places
But to a pilgrimage of the heart
And what we find
Is how strong we are
How brave
How resilient
And the deeper we go
We find who we are
We open to what is
To what may be
We find new respect for our body, mind, and spirit
We become fearless in a way
Ready to live life more fully
Open to possibilities
We become alive
In a gentle, flowing way
A way of surrendering
Surrendering to life as it is
With its heartache and darkness
With its beauty and its light

Allowing Life

There is so much letting go in this life
But in letting go
We find there is also holding on
Holding on to allowing life
To allowing joy to be a part of life
To opening to love
Opening to what is
And to what will be
For that is life
All of it
The darkness and the light
The letting go
The holding on
Life
With all its messiness
With all its beauty
We let go
We hold on

We Are One

In this life
In this world
Where so many are looking for home
So many are seeking to belong
And really
All we have to do
To be home
To belong
Is to breathe
To be in the moment
We are home
To breathe
Is to belong
We are one
All connected
By the breath
Breathing in
Breathing out
We are home
We belong
We are one

Something Called Grace

There are so many things to hold onto
Papers, pictures, things
Memories, thoughts, ideas, stuff
And the more we hold onto
The less we are connected
And yet
That is what we want
What we long for
To feel connected
But we cannot open our hearts
When we are grasping
And hanging on—we think—for dear life
What we really need to do
Is surrender and let go
And it takes great courage
To let go
But that is when we find
What we are looking for
That is when
There is something to hold onto
That is when we find
Trust and hope
And something called grace

Moments of Wonder

There are times when things seem very dark
When the questions have no answers
When the questions keep us from accepting what is
When the pain seems too deep to transcend
But then
There is a moment of wonder
A moment that gives pause to all the questions
A moment that just is
And when we let that moment in
Hope comes in too
Hope that the pain will ease
Hope that there is a way to be ok
Even with life the way it is
With its darkness
And its pain
But with its moments of wonder too
With its light
With its hope

Nothing to Hold Onto

In the letting go
You find there is nothing to hold onto
Everything changes
Everything is evolving
No matter what you do
Or don't do
Time keeps moving
The clock keeps ticking
Life goes on
It's just
Are you going to let yourself flow
Gently, constantly
Or are you going to build walls
That you bump against
Until finally they crumble
And what was held so tightly
Crashes forward with the force of the overflowing river
Forcing the letting go
And there you find
That still
There is nothing to hold onto
There is nothing to hold onto

What Is Enough

It's a hard lesson to learn
At least, for some of us
That we are enough
Just as we are
And how else could it be really?
If each of us embraced being ourselves
With our weaknesses and our strengths
With our brokenness and our healing
With our questions and our answers
Just that
If we brought who we are
In the moment
To each moment
Then
Maybe
That really would be enough

Beauty in Courage

It takes a certain kind of courage
To be happy
To keep getting up
Dusting yourself off
And trying again
To find your happy place
Again and again and again
There is a kind of beauty
In that kind of courage
The courage to smile
After the tears
The courage to always look for what is good
To find what you are grateful for
Even in loss and grief
The courage to stay
The courage to surrender
To what is
To feel the fear
And find the courage, the beauty
To be brave anyway

This Story

When the seasons are changing
Especially when winter
Is becoming spring
And there is more light
There are more birds chirping
There are buds on the trees
Tulips and daffodils peeking through the earth
It reminds me
To be grateful for this gift of life
To remember we are all a part of creation
Children of mother earth
We are a part of this story
The one about transitions
About hope and transcendence
The one about learning, growing, changing
The story about new life
About the gift of life
We are a part of this story

Words of the Heart

The heart has its own voice
Its own words
Or, at least
It has things to tell us
Things to say
And sometimes
It is good to wonder
And to wander along that path
The path of the heart
The heart that can often tell us
What we need to heal
What we need to find love
What we need to be whole
If only we could give it a voice
If only we could listen
Listen to the words
Of the heart

You Are . . . You Belong

There is an expression
"You matter because you are" *
And to take another step
You belong because you are
No need to try to fit in
No need to feel not enough
Just be
Be yourself
Because you are
And because you are
You matter
And
You belong

*Cicely Saunders

Letting the Truth In

Sometimes
We are not ready to see something
Not ready to face something
And we know we are not ready
Because we cannot process
The words
Their meaning
The emotions that come
And it doesn't mean you'll never be ready
Just not now
Not here
There's no shame in this
It just is
And your heart knows
And your mind and your body
They will protect you
From what is too much
Until you are ready
They will let a little more in
Let it work its way through
Become a part of you
And then you can see more clearly
And then
You can let the truth in

Being Ordinary

Be ordinary
That's really all we need to do
To be ourselves
To do what we are called to do
We just need to be ordinary
And in being ordinary
We can be extraordinary
We can do our part
The part that no one else can do

Lost Moments

We lose so many moments
When we are thinking about the past
Or worrying about the future
We miss what is in front of us
For it is in the little moments
That life is happening
Life is passing by
The words spoken—and not heard
The actions taken—and not seen
The love given—and not received
The need or hurt expressed—and not held
Little moments
When life is happening
The whisper
The movement
The opening
The closing
Little moments
When life is happening
So many lost moments
When life is passing by

A Question

I came across a question yesterday
"If I spend all my time watering my neighbor's garden, will my flowers grow?"
And all of a sudden
All the talk of taking care of yourself
Of boundaries
Of not doing things you'll resent
Made perfect sense
You've got to take care of your own backyard
Your own body, mind, and spirit
And then you can grow
And change
And heal

Leaving

Painful feelings
The ones we want to hide away from
The ones we try to stuff away
They need to be attended to
They have something to offer
And it seems
Once we learn
To turn toward them
Welcome them
Sit down with them
And accept what they have to give
Then
Then they can go on their way
Leaving room for something else
Leaving room for something different
Something new
Something comforting
Something to turn us around

Sometimes

In the moments we don't miss
Don't lose
Sometimes
Something strong is born
Something beautiful
Something true
In the moments we do hear
What was left unsaid
We do see
The small action
That means so much
We do receive the love
That has been given
Sometimes
We know when love is there
Right in front of us
Maybe all around us
Sometimes
We know
And we open
Just a little bit more

It All Matters II

There is a saying
"Pots and pans
Are the Buddha's body"
And it reminds me
That it matters
How we do
The things we do
Reminds me
To take care
Whether we are coming or going
Whether we are staying or leaving
Whether we are tending to small things
Or to bigger things
Take care
Because
It matters
It all matters
"Pots and pans
Are the Buddha's body . . ."

What Is Silence?

What is silence I wonder
It's certainly not
Not talking
For all the thoughts
Floating around in my head
Seem to create
Something other than silence
Even when there are no thoughts
The awareness of not thoughts
Can be pretty troubling
And then there are the other sounds
The ones that are always there
Just not noticed
Until there is "silence"
Yes
It's very curious
And I wonder
What is silence
Maybe the only true silence
Is sitting still
And listening
Really listening
To your thoughts, to another's thoughts
To the space around us
And between us

In the End

They say
In the end everything will be all right
And that,
Somehow
If it's not all right
Then it's not the end
And so
It would seem
There is a bigger story
There is something bigger than us
That can see
Perhaps
How the story ends
And how everything will be all right
If not right now
If not in this lifetime
But in the life that goes on
And life
Life always goes on

Being Lost

I've been afraid
All my life
Of being lost
And yet
It seems what I have needed
All along
Has been
To get lost
To make that my intention
Because
In order to be found
There must be
Being lost
In order to be brave
There must be being afraid
In order to be strong
There must be
Being weak
In order to be open
There must be
Being closed
And so
I surrender, to being afraid
To being weak
To being closed
To being lost

To Trust

When we decide
To trust the Universe
Trust that everything will be all right
The fear becomes palpable
The walls begin to go up
The voice gets shaky
The questions begin to rise
The tears begin to fall
Because to trust
You have to surrender
You have to let go
And what is asked of us
Is to allow the heart to open
To allow gratitude and love and laughter
To allow all of it
To allow life

Looking for Rainbows

When you have cried a river of tears
Perhaps even an ocean
And the source of those tears
Keeps filling
And refilling
That place in you
That is broken
Then maybe
Just maybe
You could look for rainbows
The symbol of promises made
Promises that everything will be all right
Someday
Some way
Somewhere
Everything will be all right

Where the Healing Begins

How do you thank someone
For holding you
When you are at your most fragile
Your most broken
When you are a mess
Mostly
You begin to heal what has hurt you
You turn around
And hold them when they are most fragile
Most broken
When they are a mess
And that is how we are one
In the brokenness
In the mess
In the holding
And in the being held
In the fragile moments of life
And in the healing
That begins from there
From the pain
From the love
From the compassion

When Courage Meets Fear

There are so many times
When we don't realize
How brave we are
Because sometimes
It is in seemingly small moments that it happens, but these are the moments
That define us
These are the moments
Where courage meets fear
And courage makes the next move
Courage asks the question
When fear would be silent
Or courage is silent
When fear would make noise
Courage stays
When fear would walk away
Sometimes courage walks away
When fear would stay
Courage lets go
When fear would hold on
And sometimes courage holds on
When fear would let go
There are so many times we have the choice
So many times we are brave
And maybe
Don't know it

Being with Time

Sometimes
It seems as if time is going by so fast
Sometimes
It seems to move so slowly
Or even to stand still
Sometimes
It seems time is running out
But time does not change its pace
It is always moving
Gently, quietly
Just as the breath moves
And if we could just be with time
Adopt its rhythm
Be with the changes
With the gentle breezes
And the storms
With the dark of night
And the light of day
The cold days
The warm days
If we could just be with time
We would be with peace
We would be with life
Life as it is

We Give What We Have

It is a hard lesson to learn
That we all give what we have to give
No more
No less
And sometimes
That is the gift
To understand
That we give what we have to give
We live, we learn
We change, we grow
And in the moments of our lives
We give what we have to give
We receive what we are able to hold
And when we know that
Know it for ourselves as well as for others
Then
There is forgiveness
Then
There is true love
For ourselves
And for others

By Example

Sometimes
Someone will come into your life
Just when you need them
They are always a light in darkness
Their life energy holds everything with love
With every act
With every word
They embody love
By their example
They give you strength to carry on
By their example
They give you hope
Hope that everything is as it needs to be
That everything will be all right
Somehow
Everything will be all right

Words

It is good to know sometimes
Where words come from
To learn their true meaning
So that
To learn that the word discipline
Is related to the word disciple
Which is to follow what you love
Gives a whole new feeling perhaps
To a word like discipline
So that
When you have discipline
It is because of love
It is because you care
It is because you are following
Following what you love

Winter in the Spring

Sometimes where we are in life
Doesn't match the season of life
Like a wintery day in the springtime
And maybe it will never match again
But there is still such beauty
So much to be grateful for
So much new life
And so
Even though there is darkness
We can always look for the light
Even though there is sadness and doubt
We can know there is joy and faith
Even though there is being broken
We can know there is being whole

We Find Our Way

Walking in the woods
You see trees of so many different ages
There are the saplings and young ones
With their smooth and tender bark
There are the older ones
With their rough and hard bark
And then there are the ancient and dying ones
With their back falling off
And their core becoming smooth and tender again
Smooth but with the nicks and marks and scars of age
And I think to myself
We are like that
There are the young ones among us
With their smoothness, their tenderness, their openness
There are the older ones
With their roughness, their hardness, their walls
And then there are the dying ones
With their wounds and scars, their tenderness, their openness
   once more
We find our way
Back to tenderness, back to openness
Through our wounds
Through our scars
We find our way
Back to love

The Question with No Answer

Yesterday
I found the dog had chewed up some of the carpet
I yelled
She cowered
I cried out why?
How could you do that?
Why would you do that?
Why?
I realized I wasn't yelling at the dog anymore
I was crying out to my son
To the Universe
Why?
My dog still cowered
I had done that to her
I had done that to myself
I was curled up on the kitchen floor
Why? Why . . . why
There was no answer coming back
Only silence
Only pain
Only shame
And then the tears
The tears that wash it all away
Until the next time
When the question that has no answer
Is spoken out loud once more

Let the Truth In

It is said
That to reject what has happened to you
Is to reject a part of yourself
So that
Until you find the strength
To surrender
The strength
To allow the truth
To be with it
Fully with it
Until you find the strength
To allow it to take you to your knees
To let the tears fall freely
And as often as they need to
Until then
There will be no healing
The darkness will stay
The light may come and go
But to find the light
To keep the light
We must first
Go to our knees
Kneel at the foot of the cross of our sorrow
And surrender
Let the truth find us
Let the truth in

Moments in Time

It is in the little things
And in the moments of our lives
That sometimes
Things fall into place
Someone gives you what they have to give
And it turns out to be just what you needed
A smile, a hug, a gift
The words you needed to hear
And it is in those moments
That your life changes
You are strong enough perhaps
Because they stayed strong for you
You have love enough
Because they held you with love
You have faith enough
Because they had faith for you
You have hope enough
Because they kept hope alive for you
And it only took a moment
But it was something to hold onto
Even as you let go

Something to Hold Onto

Something to hold onto
Even as we let go
This is the way of love
This is the way home
At least for me
Finding my way
My way to what is possible now
Now, when so much has been lost
Finding my way
To being with both the heartache and the joy
Finding my way back to life
The life that calls to me
To let go
And to hold on

Letting Go of Questions

I can let go of all the unanswered questions,
At least for now
At least I think I can
With a new understanding of the dark night of the soul
The one that says on that "night"
You lose connection with your identity
You don't know who you are
You are lost
You are not yourself
And so
When I think about my son
Standing in the field
A gun in his hand
Pulling the trigger
That was not my son
Not the son I knew
He would never have done something like that
He was lost in that moment
He was not there
The one who took my son
Was not my son
My son was away in that moment
And then
Before he found his way back
He was taken away for all time
He was taken away for all time

No Regrets When We Choose Love

Life is a sacred path
No matter how we walk it
There will be laughter
There will be struggle
It is still a sacred path
For it is one
We walk only once
And in the end
There will be no regrets
For the times we chose love
For the times we chose tenderness and compassion
Even for ourselves
Or perhaps
Especially for ourselves
For when there is love for the self
There is more love to give away
More tenderness
More compassion
There is
More love

Be Brave Enough

I read a quote the other day
"Be brave enough to break your own heart" *
And I wondered
What would that look like?
And the answer came
For me
It would be
To allow myself to be happy
And I realized how hard that would be
And how I have struggled
With even the thought
Of being happy
Or letting go
Of surrendering
Of allowing myself to be happy
And now
That is the challenge
To be brave enough
To let my heart break
To let my heart feel love
To let my heart heal
To let my heart be happy

*Cheryl Strayed

No Loopholes

There is no easy way through pain
No loopholes
No shortcuts
And sometimes
The most you can do
Is breathe
And to breathe
Is enough
Because it gets you to the next moment
The next moment
When
Maybe
There will be a place to rest
There will be a moment of peace
So
Breathe
Just breathe
And as time goes by
You will find a way
Find a way through
To where hope grows
And where hope grows
There is moving on
One breath at a time

A Way to Peace

When in the depths of despair
Some part of you
Has to know
Has to believe
That there is a way to peace
And that it takes time
There is a way to find a balance again
A way for life to go on
As it is
With the loss
With the heartache
But with love and joy as well
It's just
Sometimes
It takes a long time

Surrender to the Truth

Sometimes
I hear myself saying words
That don't feel real
My son died
My son died by suicide
My son
No, I think
That is not possible
How can I say those words
Out loud
It must be a bad dream
But there is no waking up
No way to make it go away
And so
I must lean into the pain
Surrender to the truth
And then
Start making a new story
One that holds him close
And one that lets him go
So that
Life can go on
And still be real
Still be true

Up to Us

It is said
That we can only save ourselves
Though others may support us, care about us, help us
In the end
It is up to us
To have compassion for ourselves
To see what is good
To surrender to what is
While allowing for what could be
Allowing for happiness
It is up to us
To find ways
To get back up when we are on the ground
To keep going when we are stuck
To open our hearts when they are broken
To let go while we hold on

There Is Always Good

No matter how bad things get
There is always good
The light touch of someone who loves you
The warmth of the sun
The gentle breeze
To notice these things
Sometimes
It is what you hold onto
To be able to see the stars
When there is darkness
To be able to look for the rainbow
When caught in the storm
To give meaning to the butterfly floating by
When filled with doubt
To hear a newborn cry
When all seems hopeless
There is always good
There is always good to hold onto

A Backpack of Rocks

Letting go
It seems
Is harder than holding on
But then
I think about carrying a backpack full of rocks
And really
It would be easier to put it down
And sometimes
Holding onto what is lost
Can weigh us down
Just like a backpack full of rocks
And it's hard to explain
Why we hold onto something
That feels so heavy
But at the same time
It feels like all we have
Of the one we lost
Is the feeling of loss
And it is so very hard
To let go

An Act of Courage

I have often wondered
What it is to be brave
And in the midst of great loss
It seems
It is an act of courage
To simply get up in the morning
To smile
To enjoy the simple things
It is an act of courage
To be happy
Even while carrying deep sorrow
Even while your heart is broken
It is an act of courage
To keep hope alive
Hope that there is a reason for everything
Hope that love is all you need

Day by Day

I wonder sometimes
How beauty can come from the ashes
But then I think
When a forest burns to the ground
Day by day new trees grow
Animals and birds return
Wildflowers and butterflies
And when a volcano erupts
Causing so much destruction
Day by day the earth heals itself
Flowers and plants and trees return
Beauty does come from the ashes
And in the same way
As we heal from what has taken us to the ground
From what has turned our life upside down
Day by day
We return to life
To find
Beauty is growing from the ashes

Always

We are, it seems
Always creating our story
The experiences we have
The way we process those experiences
As we let go of the past
And look to the future
It is happening every hour of every day
And as we become our story
We become authentic
We become true
We become enough

When Fear Slips In

I learned recently
That I tested positive for cancer
And I've been trying that out in my thoughts
"I have cancer"
It doesn't quite register
But then fear will slip in
What if this is the beginning of the end
What if I need to say good-bye
How will that look
How will I do that
What will I leave
I tell myself
"I'm not afraid"
And the fear slips away
To where fear goes
And then I think
This will be what it will be
It will be a part of my life
It will be a part of my story

We Are Never Alone

When fear slips in
That everything may not be all right
Then all we have to do
Is remember
Though we are alone in some ways
We are never entirely alone
For so many others have been through this
Whatever it is that we are going through
And even though, in the end
Everything may not be all right
There are many others
Who have been in this same place
Who have had these same thoughts
And so
Even in the aloneness of our experience
We are never alone

Another Day

It's amazing to me
How life goes on
And yet
This is our only life
At least
In this form
With these experiences
With this story
So it makes sense
To make the most of this life
To greet the day with gratitude
So much gratitude
That we are here
That we have another day
Another day to live and love
To experiment, to learn, to change
Another day
To be who we are
Right now
Right here
Even as we change and grow
Even
As life goes on

The Truth

One of the things I've learned
Is that
Sometimes
You just need someone to say
This really sucks
Because
Some things cannot be fixed
And all the positive thinking
And being brave
And rising up
Doesn't change that.
You just have to find ways
To carry on
To keep going
And find those who will hear your truth
And understand
Who will acknowledge your truth
Help you to carry it
So that
The weight of it is lighter
The pain of it is held more tenderly
And the waves of grief
Become softer
The waves of grief
Become more gentle

About the Arthur:

Anne is a writer, a Life Cycle Celebrant and a hospice nurse. She holds a Master's degree in Hospice Education and Bereavement. She has three children and three grand-children. She lost her youngest son to suicide. That loss often guides her in her work and her writing. Anne lives in Michigan.

www.ingramcontent.com/pod-product-compliance
Lightning Source LLC
Chambersburg PA
CBHW071118090426
42736CB00012B/1942